IMAGES
of England

THE EAST
LANCASHIRE REGIMENT
1855-1958

Francis Fuller, whose father had commanded the 59th in 1794-97, joined the Regiment in 1803 and soon saw active service at the capture of the Cape of Good Hope, 1806. He served with the 59th in the Peninsular 1812-14, including the battle of Vittoria, the capture of San Sebastian and the battles of the Nivelle and Nive. After the storming of San Sebastian, for which as the senior surviving officer of the 59th he was awarded the gold medal, Capt. Fuller wrote home: 'Our Regiment is literally cut to pieces. Nineteen officers killed and wounded. I know not how I escaped, but thank God I have come off well; a shot-hole through my cap and my breeches torn by scrambling up the breach being the only damage done to my agreeable person.' He was less fortunate at the battle of the Nive, where he was wounded in the shoulder and thigh. Fuller then served in the Waterloo campaign, including the capture of Cambrai and occupation of Paris. In 1826 he once more led the 59th into a breach, this time at the storming of the previously impregnable Indian fortress-city of Bhurtpore. For his services on this occasion, when he was again wounded, he was awarded a CB. Francis Fuller retired from the 59th in 1834 – and was succeeded in command by his younger brother.

IMAGES
of England

THE EAST
LANCASHIRE REGIMENT
1855-1958

Compiled by
Lieutenant Colonel John Downham
for The Regimental Collection of
The Queen's Lancashire Regiment

TEMPUS

First published 2000
Copyright © The Regimental Collection
of the Queen's Lancashire Regiment, 2000

Tempus Publishing Limited
The Mill, Brimscombe Port,
Stroud, Gloucestershire, GL5 2QG

ISBN 0 7524 0000 0

Typesetting and origination by
Tempus Publishing Limited
Printed in Great Britain by
Midway Clark Printing, Wiltshire

The 59th Foot under the walls of the fortress of Ghuznee, Afghanistan, after the fiercely-fought battle of Ahmed Khel, 1880. This was the last occasion on which the Regiment carried its Colours in action. In addition to showing the Colour Party, this historic eyewitness painting by Capt. J.F. Irwin of the 59th depicts the locally produced khaki uniforms of that campaign.

Contents

This Regimental Colour of the XXXth Foot, presented in 1859 and carried until 1950, almost the whole period covered by our photographs, exemplifies the continuity of Regimental life and tradition through two World Wars and many lesser conflicts.

Introduction

Early History

The East Lancashire Regiment traces its descent from two old Regiments of Foot, the XXXth and 59th. The XXXth was first raised in 1689 as Lord Castleton's Regiment to fight for William of Orange against the French and won early distinction at the capture of the fortress-city of Namur in 1695. Disbanded at the end of the war, in 1697, the Regiment was reformed in 1702 as Saunderson's Marines. The Regiment served as marines until 1713, both as detachments on board Royal Naval ships and ashore. As such they were involved in numerous battles and sieges in Spain, the Mediterranean and North Africa. The most notable of these were the capture of Gibraltar, 1704, and its subsequent defence (for which the Regiment gained its first battle honour) the naval battle of Malaga, the capture of Barcelona, Alicante, Carthagena, Majorca and Minorca, the defence of Lerida and the battle of St Estevan. The Regiment was again disbanded in 1713 but restored in 1715 as a Regiment of Foot. This was not, however, the end of marine service for the XXXth. In 1727 they were again defending Gibraltar, from 1745 to 1748 they were in the Channel Fleet, taking part in Admiral Anson's victory over the French off Cape Finiesterre in 1747, and during the Seven Years War, 1756-63, the Regiment was again embarked, raiding the French coast.

Meanwhile, in 1755 the threat of renewed war with France had resulted in the raising of several new regiments of which one was the 59th Foot. In 1782, county names were added to the numbers of Regiments of Foot, the XXXth being sub-titled 'Cambridgeshire' and the 59th '2nd Nottinghamshire' but in truth these titles had little significance in terms of either local sentiment or recruiting.

The revolt of the American colonies in 1777 found the 59th in Canada. They moved down to Boston, where they were involved in the skirmish at Lexington and the bloody battle of Bunker's Hill, following which the Regiment returned to England. Subsequently they took part in the relief of the 3rd Siege of Gibraltar. The XXXth landed in South Carolina in 1781 and later that year were engaged in the hard fought battle of Eutaw Springs. Despite this victory the war was drawing to a close and the XXXth were withdrawn to the West Indies.

Revolutionary and Napoleonic Wars

In 1793, war with Revolutionary France found Britain unprepared. The first priority was to man the Fleet and accordingly the XXXth Foot once again became marines, serving in that role for three years which included the defence of Toulon, the capture of Bastia and Calvi in Corsica (under Nelson's Command) and a naval action off Hieres. In 1798 they returned to the Mediterranean, first to Sicily and then on expeditions to capture Malta, 1800, and to wrest Egypt from the French, 1801. For their part in the battle of Alexandria the Regiment was awarded a Sphinx, superscribed 'Egypt', which was incorporated in their Colours and badges.

Meanwhile the 59th were less fruitfully employed on allied expeditions to Ostend, La Vendee, Holland (under the 'Grand Old Duke of York') and then to St Vincent, in the West Indies, where sickness was a more potent enemy than the French. Peace came in 1802 but lasted barely a year. Under the threat of invasion by Napoleon, the British Army expanded rapidly and both the XXXth and 59th raised 2nd Battalions.

Both 1st Battalions sailed for the East Indies. En route the 1/59th landed in South Africa, 1806, and assisted in the capture of Capetown from France's Dutch allies. In 1810 they left India to capture Mauritius from the French and in the next four years played a leading role in the capture of Java, Sumatra, Bali and the Celebes from the Dutch and local princes. The hard-fought battle of Cornelis in Java, 1811, stands as one of the greatest achievements in the history of the 59th Regiment.

Both 2nd Battalions served in Spain during the Peninsula War. The 2/59th took part in Sir John Moore's stand at Corunna, 1808, where it distinguished itself in a brilliant bayonet charge, and took a notable part in Wellington's victories at Vittoria, 1813, and in the Pyrenees. Its most desperate fight, however, was the storming of San Sebastian, 1813, where over 350 men fell in fierce fighting in the breach before the town was taken. The 2/XXXth suffered almost equally severe casualties in the terrible assault on Badajoz, 1812, and then shared in Wellington's victory at Salamanca where Ensign Pratt captured the Eagle of the French 22nd Regiment.

In 1815 the 2/XXXth and 2/59th joined Wellington's army for the Waterloo campaign. The 2/XXXth were at Quatre Bras, where they formed square to repel French cavalry charges, and were in the centre of the British position at Waterloo. For six hours the Battalion sustained the attacks of massed cavalry and infantry supported by murderous artillery fire. Towards the end of the day they took part in the defeat of a column of Napoleon's Imperial Guard and broke the final French attack. By early evening nearly half the Battalion had fallen and the survivors were commanded by the officer sixth in seniority, all his seniors having been killed or wounded. The 2/59th took no direct part in the battle since they were with the division guarding the right flank of the allied army, but subsequently took part in the storming of Cambrai and, with the 2/XXXth, the occupation of Paris. The campaign had a tragic sequel for the 2/59th when this gallant battalion was virtually destroyed in the shipwreck of the *Sea Horse* off the Irish coast where some 360 men, women and children were drowned. With the end of the war the remnants of both 2nd Battalions were absorbed in the 1st Battalions in India.

Soldiers of The Queen

In the century that followed Waterloo the Army was largely involved in consolidating and defending the British Empire and Regiments spent long years in overseas garrisons. Both XXXth and 59th took part in the Pindaree War in India, when the XXXth distinguished itself at the capture of the rock stronghold of Asseerghur, 1818, while in 1826 the 59th stormed the previously impregnable fortress of Bhurtpore. After a period of home service both Regiments were again posted overseas, the XXXth to Bermuda and Canada and the 59th to Gibraltar, Malta and the West Indies. Another tour of home service followed and then, in 1851 and 1850 respectively, the XXXth and 59th sailed for the Ionian islands and Hong Kong. Both were to prove eventful tours.

In 1854 the Crimean war broke out and the XXXth joined the British expeditionary force. They were in the centre of the British attack at Alma and played a prominent part in the battle of Inkerman when a two hundred of the Regiment routed three thousand Russians in a bayonet charge. For his part in this action Lt & Adjt. Mark Walker was awarded the Regiment's first Victoria Cross. The XXXth then endured the cruel Crimean winter and participated in the operations which led to the capture of Sevastopol. In 1857 the 59th took part in the capture of the Chinese city of Canton, earning a unique battle honour. These campaigns over, the XXXth moved to Gibraltar and the 59th to Capetown before returning home.

The next overseas tour for the XXXth took them to Canada where they took part in operations to repel an attempted invasion by Irish 'Fenians' from the United States, while the 59th started another long tour of garrison duty in India. In 1879/80 the 59th took part in the 2nd Afghan War and it was here that Capt. Sartorius won his Victoria Cross. At the battle of Ahmed Khel in 1880 the Regiment held the centre of the line against a furious charge of some 15,000 Afghan tribesmen. This was one of the last occasions on which a British Regiment carried its Colours in action.

In 1881 the XXXth and 59th were linked as the 1st and 2nd Battalions of the East Lancashire Regiment with a Depot at Burnley initially and then, from 1899, at Fulwood Barracks, Preston. Other constituents of the new Regiment were the Volunteer and Militia battalions, which later formed the basis of the Territorial Army. The 3rd Battalion of The East Lancashire Regiment, based in Burnley, was formed from the 5th Royal Lancashire Militia; the 1st and 2nd Volunteer Battalions (later 4th and 5th Battalions) from the 2nd and 3rd Lancashire Rifle Volunteer Corps with headquarters in Blackburn and Burnley respectively.

By the time of this amalgamation the XXXth (now 1st East Lancashires) were again serving in India, and before that tour ended they were engaged in the Chitral campaign of 1895. In 1900-02 the 1st and 3rd Battalion complete, and detachments from the Volunteers, took part in the Boer War, where the XXXth earned distinction at the battles of Karee and Zand River and in Mounted Infantry operations. Meanwhile the 2nd Battalion had embarked on another long overseas tour in India and South Africa.

The First World War, 1914-1918

In the First World War the Regiment expanded to seventeen battalions, and saw action in France and Flanders, Gallipoli, Egypt, Mesopotamia and Salonika, winning another four Victoria Crosses. It is impossible in a short précis to do justice to the gallantry and self-sacrifice displayed by the men of Lancashire in the First World War, so one example will have to suffice.

On 1 July 1916, in the opening hours of the battle of the Somme, the 1st and 11th Battalions advanced across open ground in the face of the German machine guns. Of 722 men of the 1st Battalion who went into action that day, only 237 came out while the 11th Battalion (the Accrington Pals) lost some 594 men, either killed, wounded and missing, out of a complement of 720 in the attack. This memorable devotion to duty is commemorated in the Regiment annually to this day.

Between the two World Wars, the Regular battalions of the Regiment served in Germany, Ireland, China, India, Malta, Egypt and the Sudan, Bermuda and the West Indies.

The Second World War, 1939-1945

In the Second World War, in which seven battalions of the Regiment took part, the 1st and 4th distinguished themselves in the fighting at Dunkirk, where Capt. Ervine-Andrews won his Victoria Cross. The 2nd Battalion fought in the short but brilliant action in Madagascar and in the gruelling campaign of the Arakan, then played a decisive part in the final rout of the

Japanese in Burma. The 1st and 5th fought with conspicuous gallantry in Normandy, then the old XXXth gained a formidable reputation in the great advance through France, Holland and Germany and saw the European Campaign through to its victorious end.

Peace brought reductions and in 1948 the old 'XXXth' and '59th' were at last merged to form a single Battalion. The Regiment then saw service in the Sudan, Egypt and Germany before being amalgamated in Hong Kong on 1 July 1958 with The South Lancashire Regiment (Prince of Wales's Volunteers) to form The Lancashire Regiment (Prince of Wales's Volunteers).

That is not, however, the end of the story, for today the honours and great traditions of The East Lancashire Regiment are cherished and sustained by their Regular, Territorial Army and Cadet successors of The Queen's Lancashire Regiment.

The Photographs

The great majority of the photographs in this book are from the very extensive collection in the Regimental Archives, most of them taken and donated by members of the Regiment. From the wide range of material available I have preferred to select those illustrating people, who I have named whenever possible, for the story of a great Regiment such as the East Lancashires is essentially that of ordinary people (and a few rather exceptional people) in extraordinary situations. Our Nation owes them more than it knows, and should not forget them. I have also attempted to give some impression of the diversity of roles, places and experiences, in peace and war, that have formed the rich heritage of The East Lancashire Regiment.

Acknowledgements

As compiler, I would first of all wish to acknowledge my great debt to the many past members of the Regiment, some known and others unknown, who have over the past century donated their photographs to posterity. I would also like to thank my fellow Trustees of The Regimental Collection of The Queen's Lancashire Regiment for permission to publish the photographs preserved in the Regimental Archives. Also the Imperial War Museum, Blackburn Museum and Art Gallery, and Mr C.R. Coogan for permission to reproduce those photographs marked (IWM), (Blackburn) and (Coogan Collection) respectively. Finally, I wish to thank Miss Debbie Miggins, Mr Mark Naylor and Mrs Asya Badat for their assistance in preparing this work.

One
1855-1881

Lt & Adjt. Mark Walker VC of the XXXth Regiment reading General Orders in front of his tent in the Crimea, c. April-May 1855. Walker, who was slightly wounded at the battle of the Alma and subsequently lost his arm in the trenches before Sebastopol, earned his Victoria Cross 'for daring bravery at Inkerman [5 November 1854] when, to encourage his men, he leaped over a wall in face of two battalions of Russian infantry, his regiment following and repulsing the foe.' With him, left to right, are: his soldier servant, the orderly sergeant (a Light Company NCO) and Sergeant Major John MacClellan, who was killed in the attack on the Redan, 5 September 1855.

Lt-Col. James Mauleverer CB commanded the XXXth in the Crimea, 1854-55, earning particular distinction for his gallant leadership at the battle of Inkerman. The following year he was wounded in the attack on the Redan, but returned to command his beloved Regiment in Ireland, Jersey and Canada, from where he retired in 1862. Small in stature, Mauleverer inspired strong affection and universal admiration as the best and boldest soldier in the Regiment.

The Depot of the XXXth at Parkhurst, Isle of Wight, in 1858. Left to right, front row: Capt. A.H. Williamson, Capt. W.J. Brook, Lt J. Fleming. The others are unknown. At this period Regimental depots did not have a fixed 'home' and the XXXth Depot had recently moved to the Isle of Wight from Fermoy in County Cork.

Officers of the XXXth Regiment at Richmond Barracks, Dublin, in 1858. Left to right: Capt. H.C. Singleton, Capt. C.J.P. Clarkson, Lt R.O. Campbell, Capt. L. Macpherson, Maj. R. Dillon, Maj. T.H. Pakenham MP, Capt. W.J. Brook, Maj. F.T. Atcherley. All but Dillon had served with the XXXth in the Crimea.

Quarter-guard of the XXXth Foot in aid of the civil power in Ireland during the election of 1859, which in the event passed off without undue disturbance. The officer in the centre is Ensign Octavius Boyce and on the right Capt. Lachlan 'Cluny' Macpherson.

Maj. Francis Topping Atcherley, XXXth Regiment, photographed in Jersey, *c.* 1860. Atcherley, who served in the XXXth from 1847 to 1865, commanded a company in the Crimea and distinguished himself in command of the pickets at Little Inkerman, 27 October 1854, when he was wounded and Mentioned in Despatches, and in the attack on the Redan the following September. He was described as 'A tall handsome man with a very courtly manner which was the same to all ranks and ages', and he never missed the chance of doing a kind act. His son and grandson followed him into the Regiment.

Sergeants of the XXXth Foot at South Camp, Aldershot, June 1861. Back row, left to right: C/Sgt T. Fitzgerald, Sgt J. Dolan, Sgt-Maj. W. Hunns, C/Sgt P. Ryan, Drum-Maj. J. Arthur. Middle row, standing: C/Sgt Bannen, C/Sgt M. Mulvey, Sgt Jamison, Sgt Carey, QM-Sgt M. Tooner (later QM), Sgt-Instr Musketry D. Sullivan. Front row, sitting: Sgt McWilliams, Sgt M. Ryan, Officers' Mess Sgt J. McCallam, C/Sgt J. Knoff, Sgt J. Dalgetty, C/Sgt T. Shaw, Sgt J. Taylor. Lying at the front: Hospital-Sgt H. Holmes, Sgt-Master Tailor R. Collins. On 27 June the Regiment sailed from Liverpool for Canada on Brunel's *Great Eastern*, the largest ship afloat at that time.

Officers of the XXXth Foot in Toronto, Canada, in 1862. Left to right, back row (on pillar): Capt. J.C. Hobbs, Lt M.D. Sanderson. Second row from the back: Lt W.V. Brownlow, Capt. C.J. Moorsom, Capt. L. Macpherson, Ensign J. Cooke, Ensign J. Thom. Third row: Maj. F.T. Atcherley, Ensign C.H. Garnett, Asst-Surgeon D. Milroy. Front row: Capt. A.C. Singleton, Capt. W.J. Brook, Maj. R. Dillon, Lt F.H. Williamson, Capt. H.S. Smith, Lt J. Fleming, Capt. C.J.P. Clarkson, Lt H.F. Morewood. The Regiment was in garrison at Toronto, 1861-62, Montreal, 1862-66 and, following the Fenian Raid of 1866, was based at Quebec, 1866-68 and Halifax, 1868-69.

Sergeants of the XXXth Regiment on active service in Canada during the Fenian Raid of 1866, dressed and equipped for operations on the frontier with the United States. Left to right, standing: C/Sgt M. Ryan (later Capt. and QM), Sgt T. Atkins, C/Sgt C. Dillon DCM (decorated for gallantry at the battle of the Alma in 1854), Sgt Salcombe, -?-. Seated: C/Sgt Webb, C/Sgt Smith, Sgt-Maj W. Hunns (with binoculars).

Maj. Archibald Campbell, *c.* 1860. Commissioned in 1811, and a veteran of Wellington's peninsular army, he served in the Crimea, aged sixty-five, as junior captain in the XXXth and was wounded in the attack on the Redan, 1855. Belatedly promoted, he retired as a Colonel. Both his sons served in the Regiment.

Capt. John Pennock Campbell, elder son of Archibald Campbell, photographed in Montreal in the winter uniform worn by the XXXth in Canada, *c.* 1865. As a lieutenant at the battle of Inkerman he had four or five musket balls through his clothes, one of which carried off a tail of his coat containing £9 belonging to his company. He later commanded the 1st Battalion, The East Lancashire Regiment, in India 1885-87.

Sgt Alexander Borland of the XXXth and family, *c.* 1865. Borland joined the Regiment in 1853 and served in the Crimea, where he was wounded. He was promoted to Quarter-Master-Sergeant in 1866 and Quartermaster in 1874, but died only a few years later in 1877.

Officers of the XXXth Foot at Fort Regent, Jersey, in 1872. Left to right, standing: Lt R.A. McCord, Capt. D.R. Vandaleur, Asst-Surgeon J. Paxton, Capt. H.H. Eden, Bt-Lt-Col. H.P. Hutton, Ensign A.G. Watson, Ensign H.T.P. Evans, Lt & QM M. Tooner, Ensign W. Kennady, Ensign J.M. Piercy. Sitting: Lt & Adjt. N. Bannatyne (who wrote *The History of the XXX Regiment*), Lt F. Clowes, Surgeon H. Teevan (the Regiment's first non-regimental medical officer), Col. T.H. Packenham, Lt T.R. Burns, Capt. C.H. Garnett, Capt. W.H. Clarkson, Paymaster C.M. Dawes. Tom Packenham, a nephew of the Duke of Wellington, was commissioned into the 59th in 1844 and transferred in 1850 to the XXXth, with whom he fought in the Crimea. He commanded the XXXth for nearly twelve years (1862 to 1874) and in 1890 became Colonel of The East Lancashire Regiment.

In 1849 the 59th Foot sailed for Hong Kong, remaining in that pestilent station until 1858, during which time 658 men, women and children of the Regiment had died, almost all of disease. In 1857-58 the 59th, temporarily commanded by Maj. A.E. Burmester CB (left), took part in an expedition to capture the city of Canton. Commissioned as an ensign in the 59th in 1830, Burmester subsequently commanded the Regiment (1860 to 1862) at Cape Town and Dover.

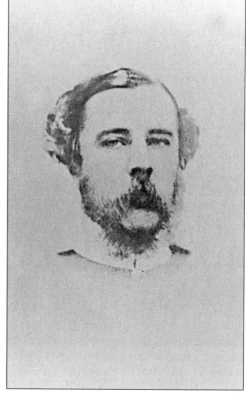

Lt & Adjt. Frederick Hackett joined the 59th Regiment in 1849. During the siege of Canton, while carrying messages, he was ambushed and beheaded by a Chinese raiding party. Next day, 29 December 1857, the 59th scaled the city walls, defended by 30,000 men and 430 cannon, to win one of the Regiment's unique battle honours.

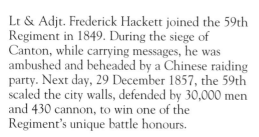

Pioneer Corporal Kitson of the 59th Regiment in full marching order with the traditional beard and axe of infantry pioneers, *c.* 1862. The Regiment was then stationed at Dover, having concluded their foreign service tour with two years in South Africa.

A private soldier of the 59th Foot wearing his 'walking out' uniform, *c.* 1862. His shell jacket has white Regimental facings and the 59th were nicknamed 'the Lilywhites' – supposedly a tribute to their smart appearance during Sir John Moore's gruelling retreat to Corunna in 1809, a tradition borne out by the Regiment's disciplined performance in the subsequent battle.

The Sergeants of the 59th Regiment at Aldershot, *c.* 1864. (Coogan Collection)

The Corps of Drums of the 59th Foot, probably at the Curragh Camp, near Dublin, in 1866. The Drum Major, unaccountably, is from the 47th Regiment who were, at that time, with the XXXth in Canada. In 1867 the Regiment sailed to Columbo, Ceylon, to begin thirteen years of foreign service.

Gen. Henry Eyre, the last Colonel of the 59th Regiment, 1865-81. He was also the last serving officer to have been commissioned as a child, having become an ensign at the age of eleven.

The Officers of the 59th Regiment in India, *c.* 1869. The Regiment landed at Bombay in March that year and were quartered at Wanowrie Barracks, Poona, until the following March when they marched to Mhow. (Coogan Collection)

The 59th Foot at Agra, India in 1875. The Regiment served in that station from 1874 to 1876.

The Band of the 59th Regiment at Dagshai, India in 1877. The following year the 59th marched out of barracks to the tune *Far Away* to take part in the Second Afghan War (1878-80).

Capt. A. Powys, 59th Regiment, who died of disease in 1879 when in charge of a cholera camp at Kandahar in Afghanistan. Powys, who also served with the Regiment in Ceylon and India, was an enthusiastic sportsman and on one big game hunting expedition he saved the life of a brother officer with the last bullet in his pouch.

Euston Henry Sartorious VC served in the 59th, 1862-81. He was a captain when awarded the Victoria Cross for assaulting a hill at Shahjui in Afghanistan, 24 October 1879, routing its fierce defenders in hand-to-hand combat. He was later to become Colonel of The South Lancashire Regiment, 1909-21.

Capt. C.V.S. Downes of the 59th, photographed at Kabul in 1880 wearing locally made 'khaki' field uniform and an early version of the 'Sam Browne' belt.

Officers of the 59th Regiment wearing local dress during the Afghan war of 1878-80. The 59th were involved in a number of actions including the battles of Ahmed Khel and Urzoo.

Sergeants of the XXXth at Dover Citadel, 1879, wearing the new home service helmet with brass spike that had replaced the shako only the previous year. Left to right, at the front: Sgt-Maj. Sanderson, Lt-Col. H.P. Hutton, Drum-Maj. T. Butler. The others are unknown.

Officers of the XXXth Foot at Ranikhet, India in 1881. Left to right, back row, standing: Capt. A.G. Watson, Capt. A.J.A. Wright. Middle row, standing: Lt C.A. Bray, 2nd-Lt E.H.F. Finch, Lt J.E. Robinson, 2nd-Lt R.T. Crowther, 2nd-Lt H.L. Gallwey, 2nd-Lt H.M. Browne, Paymaster J.J. Morris, Capt. C.R. Hornby, Lt F.S. Derham. Seated: Capt. J.E. Goodwyn, Lt W.G. Hamilton, Maj. B.C. Becher (Staff), Lt-Col. C.J. Moorsom, Gen. A.W. Murray (GOC), Maj. J.P. Campbell, Maj. F.H. Williamson. Front row, seated on ground: 2nd-Lt C.J. Morse, 2nd- Lt H.A. Browning, 2nd- Lt C.R.M. O'Brien, 2nd-Lt C. de B. Martindale. On 1 July that year the Regiment was linked to the 59th Foot, becoming 1st Battalion The East Lancashire Regiment – though the old title lingered unofficially until after the Second World War.

The Officers of 2nd Lancashire Rifle Volunteer Corps, c. 1870. This Corps, raised in Blackburn in 1859, was the second oldest in the County. It was linked to the XXXth and 59th in 1873, became 1st Volunteer Battalion The East Lancashire Regiment, in 1890 and then, on formation of the Territorial Force in 1908, re-titled 4th Battalion, The East Lancashire Regiment.

The Band of 2nd Lancashire Rifle Volunteer Corps in camp at Clevelys, 1868. The bandsmen at that time wore white uniforms.

A shooting team of the Burnley-based 3rd Lancashire Rifle Volunteer Corps, 1872. Formed in 1861, this unit became 2nd Volunteer Battalion, The East Lancashire Regiment, in 1890 and, from 1908, the 5th Battalion The East Lancashire Regiment.

The Officers of 2nd Lancashire Rifle Volunteer Corps and their ladies in camp at Clevelys, 1879.

Two
1881-1899

Officers of 1st Battalion, The East Lancashire Regiment, at Ferozepore, 1885. Left to right, back row: Lt E.H.F. Finch, Capt & Paymaster G.C. Robotham, Maj F. Clowes, Capt C.S. Cumberland, Lt F.S. Derham, Capt W.H. Scott, Lt H.E. Browne, Lt Swinburn, Lt T. Capper. Second row from the back: Capt. P. Evans, Lt W.G. Hamilton, Capt. A.G. Watson, Lt H.M. Twynam (these last two were mentioned in despatches for gallantry with the 59th at Ahmed Khel). Third row, seated: Lt E.R. Reade, Lt C.J. Morse, Col. J.P Campbell, Col. C.J. Moorsom (his arm in a sling from a serious wound at Sebastopol thirty years before), Maj. F.H. Williamson, Capt. A. Bray. Front row, seated on ground: Lt L.L. Pile, Lt A. Giles, Lt C.R.M. O'Brien.

Sergeants of 1st Battalion, The East Lancashire Regiment (the former XXXth Foot), at Ferozepore, 1887.

'F' Company, 1st Battalion, The East Lancashire Regiment, at Benares in 1890.

The Regimental Polo team, Ferozepore, 1888. The polo shirts and caps were in the XXXth Regimental colours, maroon, primrose and black, which were adopted in 1879 and used for a wide range of Regimental sportswear and 'mufti' items, including ties, blazers, cricket caps and hat ribbons. These colours were subsequently adopted by the East Lancashire, the Lancashires and (with Lincoln green substituted for primrose) the present Queen's Lancashire Regiment.

A Mess bungalow at Ferozepore, 1887, typical of those shared by junior officers such as the group pictured outside with their horses and servants.

Officers of the 1st Battalion, The East Lancashire Regiment, at Ferozepore, 1888. The Colours, presented to the XXXth Foot in Phoenix Park, Dublin in 1859, were carried by the Battalion until 1950, by which time they were the oldest still carried in the British Army.

Staff Sergeants of the XXXth Regiment at Lucknow, c. 1893. Left to right, back row: Canteen Sgt Eli Alderson, Armourer-Sgt William Holmes, QMS (Orderly Room Sgt) Sidney Williamson, C/Sgt (Pay-Master Sgt) William Butler, RQMS William Green, Sgt-Master Tailor William Russell, Sgt-Drummer David Carnell. Middle row: Band Master Frederick Russell, Sgt-Maj. Arthur McAra (died on the Malakand campaign of 1895), School Master William Cooper. Front row: Band Sgt Thomas Busby, Pioneer Sgt Thomas Bourne.

Medical staff and orderlies of the 1st East Lancashires who served through the terrible cholera epidemic of 1894 at Kokrail, near Lucknow, when the battalion suffered 145 cases resulting in 93 deaths. The XXXth bore its misfortune with great discipline and fortitude, and there was no shortage of volunteers willing to risk their own lives to tend the sick. 'Kokrail 1894' brought as much honour, and sorrow, to the Regiment as any of the battle honours emblazoned on its Colours.

The cholera cemetery and memorial of the 1st Battalion, The East Lancashire Regiment, at Kokrail, near Lucknow. On the left is LCpl Davis who volunteered to dig the cholera graves when the local staff ran away from the pestilence. On retirement this regimental 'character', better known as 'Joe Banks', held the distinction of being the senior Lance Corporal in the British Army.

Signallers of the 1st Battalion, The East Lancashire Regiment, with heliograph equipment, lamps and semaphore flags, probably at Lucknow, *c*. 1895. The Signals Officer is Lt F.H. Trent and his Sergeant, seated on left, is Sullivan. (Blackburn)

Maj. Archibald Wright (Second-in-Command of the 1st Battalion, The East Lancashire Regiment) with his wife, daughter and khidmatgar (with silver regimental badge in his pagri) at their bungalow in Lucknow, *c*. 1895.

The 1st Battalion, The East Lancashire Regiment, on parade at Lucknow, 1895, before departing for the Malakand campaign on the turbulent North West Frontier of India where they earned the battle honour 'Chitral'. The three mounted officers are, left to right: Maj. W.H. Scott, Maj. A.J.A. Wright, Capt. & Adjt L. Head.

Camps in the Malakand Pass occupied by the 1st Battalion, The East Lancashire Regiment, during the Chitral relief expedition of 1895.

Officers and Sergeants of the detachment of the 1st Battalion, The East Lancashire Regiment, at Meiktila, Burma, in 1897. Left to right, front row: Provost-Sgt Bennett, CSgt Millett, Capt. & Adjutant Baumgartner, Maj. W.H. Scott (OC), Lt W.H. Traill, Sgt J. Ferguson. Second right, back row is Sgt-Drummer P. Lydon (wearing Sam Browne belt). The others are unknown. James Ferguson enlisted in the East Lancashire Regiment at Blackburn in 1888, aged sixteen, and served for twenty-eight years, being discharged on pension in 1916. Rejoining within months, he ended his service in 1919 as a Captain. Ferguson took part in many campaigns, and was mentioned in Lord Kitchener's South African despatches, 1902, and by GOC, 42nd East Lancashire Division, for gallantry at Gallipoli in 1915. His three brothers, five nephews and his son all served in the Regiment. Pat Lydon, who later became Regimental Sergeant Major, was, like Ferguson, from a Regimental family. His grandfather, Pte Luke Lydon, was with the 30th at the storming of Badajoz in 1812, and subsequently, as a Sergeant, became Regimental Schoolmaster. His father, Sergeant Dominick Lydon, was wounded with the Regiment at the battle of the Alma in the Crimea, 1854. (Blackburn)

A musical entertainment by officers and ladies of the XXXth at Meiktila, Burma, *c.* 1897. (Blackburn)

An Officers' Mess tea party, 1st Battalion, The East Lancashire Regiment, at Meiktila, *c.* 1897. (Blackburn)

Officers of the 1st Battalion, The East Lancashire Regiment, at Portsmouth wearing undress home service uniform, 1898. Left to right, standing: Capt. & Adjt. L. St G. Le Marchant, Maj. B.G. Lewis, Lt J.S.J. Baumgartner, Lt H.L. Wethered. Seated: Lt-Col. A.J.A. Wright.

Sergeants of the 1st Battalion, The East Lancashire Regiment, at Portsmouth, March 1898. From left to right, at the back: Pioneer-Sgt Cox, Sgt Richardson. Second row from the back: Sgt Sisson, Sgt Woods, Sgt Lawrence Sgt Bull. Third row: CSgt Mottershead, Sgt-Drummer Lydon, Signals Sgt Beeson, Mess Sgt Woodbine, Sgt Jones, Sgt Burgess, Sgt Ferguson, Sgt Irwin, Sgt Oxford, Sgt Bell, Band-Sgt Ablett. Fourth row: Sgt-Master Tailor Going, Armourer-Sgt Evans, Sgt Akhurst, Sgt Quinland, Sgt Sharkey, Sgt Harrison, CSgt Connor, Sgt Holmes, Sgt Harding, Sgt Crossley. Front row: CSgt White, CSgt Mackenzie, Sgt Mathewson, Sgt-Master Cook Cates, Capt. & Adj. L. Head, Lt-Col. H.T.P. Evans, Sgt-Maj. Butler, QMS Williamson, Mr Cawte, CSgt Sullivan, Sgt Millett.

The Regimental Cricket XI at the United Services Ground, Portsmouth, in 1898. Left to right, back row: -?- (umpire), Sgt Coxon, Sgt Oxford, Capt. F.H. Trent, Lt G.E.M. Hill, Lt E.R.P. Boileau, Sgt Ashurst, Pte Pike (scorer). Front row: Capt. G.H. Lawrence, Maj. A.J.A. Wright, Capt. H.M. Browne, Capt. L. Head, Lt H.L. Wethered.

The 2nd East Lancashires football team, winners of the Governor's Cup, at Gibraltar in 1893/94. Left to right, back row: Sgt Spicer (trainer), Sgt Parker, Pte Entwistle, Pte Everett, Pte Ward, Lt Tweedie (honorary secretary and linesman). Middle row: Pte Tobin, Pte Bryce, Pte Harwood. Front row: Cpl Lewis, Pte McGuiness, Lt Wethered (captain), Pte Chalmers, Pte Murray. A white fleur-de-lys was the badge of the old 59th Regiment and was invariably used on 2nd Battalion sports strips.

Subaltern officers of the 59th at play, possibly at Gibraltar where the Battalion served from January 1893 to April 1895. Amateur theatricals were a popular pastime throughout the Army, particularly in overseas stations.

Officers of the 59th at mess during manoeuvres in 1895 or 1896, after the Battalion arrived in Aldershot from Gibraltar to join the 1st Infantry Brigade. The officers are wearing red home service tunics and white tropical helmets.

The mounted officers of the 2nd Battalion, The East Lancashire Regiment, at Aldershot, c. 1895-97. Left to right: Maj. Watson (Second-in-Command), Lt-Col. Evans (Commanding), Lt & Adjt. H.L. Wethered.

Pioneers of the 59th in red serge field service uniform, at Aldershot, with what the original caption terms a 'phizzer-man' – selling sherbet drinks, c. 1895-97. The kneeling sergeant is carrying a saw-edged pioneer sword in addition to his axe.

The 59th march past with rifles at the trail in Aldershot, headed by the Pioneers and the Band

The Regimental Band and Corps of Drums of the 2nd Battalion, The East Lancashire Regiment, nicknamed 'The Lilywhites' or 'The 5 and 9s', at Aldershot, c. 1895-97. To the far

and Drums, c. 1895-97.

right of this group are the Bandmaster and Drum Major, and a pioneer stands far left.

An ammunition mule of the 59th at Aldershot, *c.* 1895-97. Two mules per battalion were used in action to carry reserve ammunition forward from the unit's four small-arms ammunition carts to the firing line.

The 59th (in white helmets) street-lining in London at Queen Victoria's Diamond Jubilee, 22 June 1897, as troops from throughout the British Empire march past. The Battalion lined the route from Hyde Park Corner to the western end of Constitution Hill. In September that year the Battalion sailed for India.

Guard mounting by the 59th at Ranikhet in northern India, c. 1898-99.

The 2nd Battalion, The East Lancashire Regiment, on parade at Ranikhet with the Pioneers, Drums and Band to the left, 1898.

Sergeants of the Blackburn-based 2nd Lancashire Rifle Volunteers at Clitheroe, 1887. For many years they held their Annual Dinner there at The White Lion.

The Officers of the 1st Volunteer Battalion, The East Lancashire Regiment, wearing mess kit in camp at Blackpool, 1892.

Three
1899-1914

Officers of the 1st Battalion, The East Lancashire Regiment, on mobilization for the Boer War at Aldershot, December 1899. Left to right, back row: Capt. E.A. Daubeny, Capt. E.E. Coventry. Second row from the back: Capt. L.C.B. Hamber, Lt E.C. Da Costa, Capt. F.H. Trent, the Regimental Medical Officer, Capt. G.H. Lawrence, Lt R.A. Gosset, Lt R. Forrester, 2nd-Lt E.J. Wolseley, Capt. G.E. Sharp. Third row, seated: Capt. L. Head, Maj. C.R.M. O'Brien, Capt. & Adjt L. St G. Le Marchant, Lt-Col. A.J.A. Wright, Maj. B.G. Lewis, Capt. H.M. Browne, Capt. L.L. Pile. Front row: Lt P.C.W. Goodwyn, Lt & QM W. Holbourn, Lt F.J.O. Bonnyman, 2nd-Lt G. Clayhills.

The 1st East Lancashires embarking at Southampton for the Cape, 13 December 1899.

Pte 'Chuckles' Clowes DCM joined the XXXth at Lucknow in November 1892 and served in India and Burma, including the Chitral Campaign of 1895. At Karee, Pte Clowes was moving ahead of his Company as a scout and had nearly reached the Boer position on a kopje when they opened fire on him. Remarkably, he was not hit as he ran back to report to his Company. He rejoined his section and advanced with it. When Pte Birtwistle, a Burnley man and another veteran of India, was mortally wounded, he went to his assistance and stood up while hauling him under cover. One bullet went through Clowes' water-bottle, then another through both his forearms. Clowes was awarded a Distinguished Conduct Medal. He was eventually induced to go for promotion and was Machine Gun Sergeant when invalided out of the Regiment in 1911 as a result of his old wounds.

The 1st Battalion, The East Lancashire Regiment, in action at the battle of Karee, north of Bloemfontein, 29 March 1900, where they took the key to the Boer position at the cost of five men killed and ten wounded. The Battalion then took part in Lord Roberts' 'Great Advance' to capture Johannesburg and Pretoria.

Lt G.C.D. Kempson, the 1st Battalion, The East Lancashire Regiment, wearing foreign service uniform on departure for the Boer War, c. 1900. The Regiment did not in fact carry swords in South Africa. Kempson later served with the Regiment in the First World War.

Volunteers from among the officers and men of the East Lancashire Volunteer Battalions formed a succession of Active Service Companies to serve with the 1st Battalion in South Africa. Left to right, back row: Pte Baron, Pte O. Cartmell, Lt W. Fisher, Pte W.E. Mathews. Front row: Pte T. Webster, Pte C. Whitehead, Pte F. Wilson.

The first Camp in South Africa of the East Lancashires' 1st Active Service Company, *c.* March 1900. The Volunteers were at first stationed at Laingsburg and tasked with security duties on the Cape to Kimberley railway, but later joined their 1st Battalion at Johannesburg.

An East Lancashire sentry on guard at a Rand gold mine near Johannesburg, where the 1st Battalion were in garrison from May 1900 to April 1901 before resuming more active operations with mobile columns.

Reading letters from home: East Lancashires at Wilkop in the Transvaal, 1900. It was a great letter-writing age and the Regimental archives contain many personal accounts of the Boer War.

East Lancashire Mounted Infantry in South Africa, 1900. British soldiers soon became as adept as the Boers at living off the land, and this soldier has returned from a foraging expedition with a plump goose across his saddle bow.

Officers of the East Lancashire Company, 8th Mounted Infantry probably in 1902. Left to right, back row, standing: Lt E.J. Wolseley, Lt A.C. Aubin. Front row, seated: Lt G. Clayhills DSO, Capt. E.R. Collins (OC), Lt P.C.W. Goodwyn DSO. The Company was in constant contact with the enemy and acquired a formidable reputation for its daring exploits.

Preparing Christmas Dinner on the South African veldt, 1900. The staple diet 'on trek' was bully beef and ration biscuit.

Volunteers of the East Lancashire Regiment leaving South Africa for home aboard the *Avondale Castle*, 1901.

The Officers and NCOs of 'A' Company, 2nd Battalion, The East Lancashire Regiment, Dalhousie, India, 24 June 1901.

'B' Company, 2nd Battalion, The East Lancashire Regiment, bridge-building on detachment at Kasauli, India, May 1901. The Battalion Headquarters were at Jullundur.

Dmr Henry Hargreaves (standing) of the 59th, at Poona, *c.* 1905. Note that both men are wearing South African War ribbons, marksmanship badges and service stripes. Hargreaves was killed in action, as a Sergeant of 1st Battalion, The East Lancashire Regiment, in the devastating attack at Beaumont Hamel on the Somme, 1 July 1916.

The 2nd Battalion, The East Lancashire Regiment, on parade in company column with Band, Drums and transport to the left, Poona, 1907.

The 59th on parade, probably at Poona, *c.* 1903-07.

The Band, 2nd Battalion, The East Lancashire Regiment, Karachi, 1908-09. Note the young band boys.

The Best Shooting Company, 2nd Battalion, The East Lancashire Regiment, Karachi, 1908-09.

The Irish Brigade: 'D' Company, 2nd Battalion, The East Lancashire Regiment, winners of the Lambert Cup for inter-company Swedish Drill, Mhow, Central India, 1911. The 59th always recruited many Irishmen, so much so that their 'D' Company was traditionally known as 'The Irish Brigade'; hence the shamrock on their vests.

The 2nd Battalion, The East Lancashire Regiment, on the march, South Africa, *c.* 1912-14.

A company pay parade in South Africa. Note the diamond helmet flash, initially worn by the 59th from around 1908, but subsequently adopted throughout the East Lancashire Regiment and by their successors.

Soldiers of the 59th in bivouac near Cape Town, South Africa, *c.* 1912.

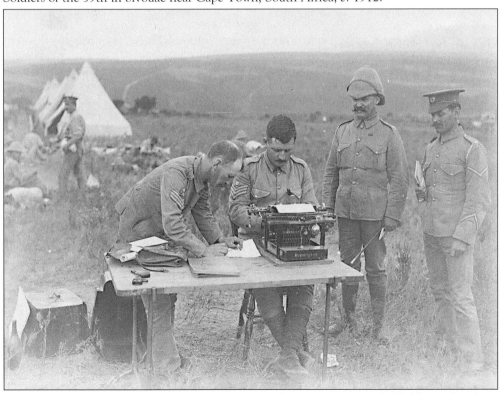

The Orderly Room, 2nd Battalion, The East Lancashire Regiment, in the field, South Africa, *c.* 1912.

Officers of the XXXth at Portobello Barracks, Dublin, in 1903. Left to right, back row, standing: Capt. G.D. Leake, Bt-Maj. F.H. Trent, Lt H.L. Wethered, 2nd-Lt A.St.L. Goldie, Capt. E.F. Rutter, Lt G.C.D. Kempson, Capt. E.R. Collins DSO, Lt E.E. Coventry, Capt. A.A. Sanders. Middle row, seated: Capt. L.C.B. Hamber, Capt. L.St.G. Le Marchant DSO, Maj. F.S. Derham, Lt-Col. B.G. Lewis DSO, Capt. & Adjt E.C. Da Costa, Bt-Maj. E.A. Daubeny, Capt. W.H. Cooper. Front row, seated on ground: 2nd-Lt E.T. Mansfield, 2nd-Lt P.O.E. d'Esterre, Lt O.B. Hargreaves.

Capt. & Adjt E.C. Da Costa with the Corps of Drums XXXth at Dublin, c. 1903-06. The Drums are wearing the German-style Brodrick cap, an unpopular form of headdress that did not long survive.

Winners of the Dublin Garrison Cup, 1904. This exceptionally strong XXXth cricket team went through the season undefeated. From left to right, back row: Sgt-Dmr A.E. Goose, Bandsman Williams, Sgt Waring, Sgt Coxon, Sgt Martin. Middle row: Lt Wethered, Capt. Rutter, 2nd-Lt Goldie, 2nd-Lt Hornby. Front row: 2nd-Lt Mansfield, 2nd-Lt Hargreaves, S/Sgt Orr.

The 1st Battalion, The East Lancashire Regiment, re-enact the crossing of a South African spruit at a Military Tournament, Ballsbridge, Dublin, 1905.

The Quartermaster's Wedding: the marriage of Lt. S.H. Williamsom, 1st Battalion, The East Lancashire Regiment, and Rachael, daughter of Lt-Gen. Ross, late Bengal Cavalry, at Aldershot, 30 August 1905. Sidney Williamson had served eighteen years in the ranks before being commissioned. During the First World War he was Quartermaster at the Depot.

Officer Commanding and Sergeants of 'C' Company, 1st East Lancashires, winners of the Inter-Company Shooting Shield and Sergeants' Cup, 1908. Left to right, back row, standing: Sgt Glasford, Sgt Huntly. Front row, seated: Sgt Ashcroft Sgt Quinland, Capt. Maclear, CSgt Yarwood, Sgt Phillips. The period before the First World War was something of a golden age of Army shooting, enabling the British Infantry to astonish their enemies in 1914 with the rapidity of their aimed rifle fire.

A detachment of 'F' Company, 1st East Lancashires, commanded by Capt. Rutter, marching at ease while taking part in the 1909 Evelyn Wood Competition. The Battalion was stationed at Woking, 1908-11, then moved to Colchester.

The Corporals, 1st Battalion, The East Lancashire Regiment, Colchester, 1912. Typical of the 'Old Contemptibles', these were the men who fought and in many cases died in the battles of 1914 and early 1915. Their high standard of training, particularly in musketry, led to the British Expeditionary Force being described as 'a rapier among scythes'.

The 1st Battalion, The East Lancashire Regiment, at Colchester, *c*. 1912-14. The Battalion

mobilized there in August 1914. (Blackburn)

The Sixteenth Annual Dinner of The East Lancashire NCOs' and Men's Dinner Club at the Holborn Restaurant, London, was attended by 114 members, including some 50 to 60 from the 1st Battalion, under the chairmanship of Sgt-Maj. P. Lydon. Button-holes were presented by the President of the Club, Col. W.J. Frampton, who was among the sixteen officers who joined the party after this photograph for toasts, speeches and a concert. The Dinner Club, founded in 1893, is believed to be the oldest such Regimental Association in the British Army.

The regimental journal of the XXXth, and invaluable historical record, was first published at Ranikhet, northern India, in August 1880. The 59th Regiment also published a very early newspaper, called *The Sentinel*, from 1879.

The Depot of The East Lancashire Regiment, Fulwood Barracks, Preston, September 1912. The back three rows are unnamed. Left to right, Fourth row from the back: Cpl Waller, Cpl Spencer, Cpl Astley, Cpl Goodall, Cpl Cramer, Cpl Sayers, Cpl Barnes, Cpl Morris, Cpl Halliday, Cpl Rolfe. Fifth row: Sgt Wallace, Sgt Haslam, Sgt Shipway, Sgt R. Woodman, Sgt Hagan, Sgt Carroll, Sgt Dawson, Sgt Bennett, Sgt G. Woodman, Sgt Hayes. Sixth row: Sgt-Dmr Goody, CSgt Donagh, CSgt Jackson, CSgt Martin, CSgt Watkins, CSgt Johnson, CSgt Sutherland, CSgt Cunliffe, CSgt Buckle, CSgt McDonald. Seventh row, seated: Sgt-Maj. Davidson, Lt H.M. Warner, Capt. G.T. Seabroke, Capt. E.F. Rutter, Maj. G.H. Lawrence (OC), Lt & Adjt W. Orr Paterson, Capt. G.D. Leake, Capt. & QM S.H. Williamson, Lt F.M. Livingston-James. Front row: Dmr Strange, LCpl Smith, Dmr Blackburn, Dmr Fullerton, Dmr Gettins, Dmr Pinner, Dmr Hurst.

The Officers of the 3rd (Militia) Battalion, The East Lancashire Regiment, at Annual Camp in a variety of field, working and ceremonial dress, 1906. The Battalion had seen active service in South Africa 1900-01 but was destined, like all Militia battalions, to lose its operational status in 1908 and become a draft-finding and training Special Reserve battalion, a role it fulfilled throughout the First World War.

The detachment of the 1st Volunteer Battalion, The East Lancashire Regiment, which attended the Coronation of King Edward VII, 1902.

Officers of the 1st Volunteer Battalion, The East Lancashire Regiment, relaxing outside their mess tent in camp at Scarborough, 1907. Note the fashionable 'Boer War' hat affected by the gentleman in civilian clothes.

'The Last Muster' of the 1st Volunteer Battalion, The East Lancashire Regiment, March 1908, when in consequence of Haldane's reform of the Reserve Forces they became 4th Battalion, The East Lancashire Regiment. The Battalion became part of the East Lancashire Division, which in 1915 was re-named 42nd Division, and fought with that Territorial Division in both World Wars.

Presentation of Colours to the 4th Battalion, The East Lancashire Regiment, by HM King Edward VII, 6 July 1909. Left to right, back row, standing: Sgt J.T. Finn. Lt G.H. Lewis, CSgt G. Burgess, Lt S.B. Norwood, Sgt J.T. Shipstone. Front row, seated: Lt-Col. F.D. Robinson VD, Lt-Col. J. Johnston VD, Lt-Col. T.H. Wesley TD.

Junior Cadets of Stonyhurst College Cadet Corps, July 1905, wearing South African-style slouch hats. The Corps, formed in 1860, became affiliated to the East Lancashire Regiment in 1900 and has produced many of the Regiment's most distinguished officers. (Blackburn)

Four
1914-1918

The Sergeants of the 1st Battalion, The East Lancashire Regiment, on mobilization in August 1914.

On 18 August 1914 the 1st Battalion, The East Lancashire Regiment, entrained at Colchester and moved to Harrow, where the 4th Division was concentrated. This photograph of the Battalion on parade, over 1,000 strong, was taken prior to departure for France on 21 August. Most of these men, the immortal 'Old Contemptibles' were killed or wounded within weeks. In January 1915 Brig.-Gen. Hunter-Weston, their brigade commander, wrote of the Battalion: 'They had died but never given way, and they had acted up to the highest traditions of the British Army. There could be no higher praise'.

The Officers of the 1st Battalion, The East Lancashire Regiment, on embarkation for France, August 1914. From left to right, back row: 2nd-Lt W.A. Salt, 2nd-Lt R.Y. Parker, Lt F.D. Hughes, Lt H.T. McMullen, Capt. A.St.L. Goldie, Lt E.M.B. Delmege, Lt J.F. Dyer, Lt W.E. Dowling, Lt N.A. Leeson, Lt H.W. Canton, 2nd-Lt W.R. Tosswill. Middle row: Capt. Walker (ASC), Capt. E.E. Coventry, Capt. G. Clayhills DSO, Lt & Adjt F.E. Belchier, Maj. T.S. Lambert, Lt-Col. L.St.G. Le Marchant DSO, Maj. E.R. Collins DSO, Maj. J.E. Green, Capt. G.T. Seabrooke, Lt & QM R. Longstaff. Front row: 2nd-Lt G.H.T. Wade, Lt C.E.M. Richards, 2nd-Lt K. Hooper, 2nd-Lt T.H. Mathews, Lt E.C. Hopkinson, Lt W.M. Chisolm, Lt R.A. Flood (RAMC). Of the twenty-six East Lancashires in this photograph, nine were killed and twelve wounded.

The first wartime regimental wedding at Plymouth on 24 August 1914. The uniformed officers are, left to right, back row: Maj. J.H. Anderson (59th), Capt. W.J.C. Luddington (59th), Capt. L.A. Cane, the best man (59th), Lt & QM H. Naylor (59th), Lt-Col. C.J. Lloyd Carson (CO, 3rd Battalion), and Lt F.H. Bellamy (3rd Battalion). Front row: 2nd-Lt F.E.C. Lewis (XXXth), Capt. & Adjt W. Orr-Paterson (59th), Lt H.M. 'Plum' Warner, the groom (XXXth). The bridegroom was under orders to join the 1st Battalion in France where, within weeks, both he and his best man were killed in action. His poor bride died of grief.

The 1st Battalion, The East Lancashire Regiment, 'somewhere in France', 24 August 1914. They are seen at a halt on their train journey to join the British Expeditionary Force. On detraining at Le Cateau they heard the news that: 'There's the hell of a German army marching round our flank,' and were in action there on 26 August. (Blackburn)

Lt E.C. Hopkinson MC, 1st Battalion, The East Lancashire Regiment, after the epic 'Retreat from Mons'. He had earned his Military Cross a few days earlier in the Battalion's gallant rearguard action at the battle of Le Cateau. To his left rear, with stick, is Capt. Clayhills, killed on 2 November during heavy fighting near Ploegsteert. (Blackburn)

In the trenches at Le Gheer, near Ploegsteert early in 1915. This area was held by the 1st Battalion, The East Lancashire Regiment, for over six months from 21 October 1914 (when the Battalion counter-attacked to capture the position) until the end of April 1915. Seen are, left to right: Sgt Woodger, Lt W.Y. Paton MC (wounded at Ypres, May 1915), Cpl Kirk.

The Convent at Le Gheer, February 1915. Within some 300yds of the German trenches, this was a company headquarters for nearly six months. Left to right: Lt (late WO II) Wilkinson, Lt C.E.M. Richards, 2nd-Lt C. Waddington.

A view from the 1st East Lancashire trenches at Shell Trap Farm towards the burning town of Ypres, c. 11 May 1915. The soldier in the foreground is in the line of shallow trenches and breastworks which the Battalion defended between 9 and 15 May during the Second Battle of Ypres at a cost of 17 officers and 370 other ranks, including many of the surviving pre-war Regulars.

The Officers of the 59th on mobilization at Wynberg, near Cape Town, August 1914. Left to right, back row: 2nd-Lt A.H. Penny, Lt R.S. Boothby, Capt. G.B. Newcomen, Lt (QM) Shaw. Middle row: Lt B.W. Molony, Lt T.H. Daw, Lt G.A. Seckham, Lt G.W.V. Hoskyn, Capt. B.C.M. Western, Capt. G.M. Smith, 2nd-Lt I.V. Townsend, 2nd-Lt E.A.M. Larkins, 2nd-Lt C.H. Martin, Lt A.B. Thompson. Front row: Capt. C. Fletcher, Capt. L. Russell, Maj. A.A. Sanders, Maj. H. MacClear, Lt-Col. C.L. Nicholson, Capt. K.H.L. Arnott (Adjutant), Capt. W.F. Richardson, Capt. T.E. Skewes-Cox.

A group of Sergeants of the 59th aboard the *Dover Castle* bound from Cape Town to take part in the First World War. Left to right, back row: Synott, Duckworth, Carefoot, Miller, Bright, Wilson, Benton, Morgan. Middle row: Hearney, Price, Webster, Quigley, O'Hara. Front row: -?-, -?-, Nicholson, Gerrity, Adams, Martin, Sharples.

Mobilization of the 4th Battalion, The East Lancashire Regiment, at their Canterbury Street headquarters, Blackburn, on 5 August 1914. The Battalion consisted of Territorials from Blackburn, Clitheroe and Darwen. (Blackburn)

Lt Bob Thwaites and his Machine Gun Section of the 4th Battalion, The East Lancashire Regiment, on route to Egypt aboard RMS *Deseado*, September 1914. (Blackburn)

A Guard found by the 4th Battalion, The East Lancashire Regiment, presents arms at the Citadel of Cairo, garrisoned by the Battalion from September 1914 until April 1915, when they embarked for Gallipoli. The Regiment had last occupied this Citadel in 1801 when the French surrendered it to the XXXth Foot. (Blackburn)

Officers of the 4th Battalion, The East Lancashire Regiment, pictured at the Citadel Barracks, Cairo, in December 1914. Left to right, back row: Lt I.L. Simpson, Lt R. Thwaites, Capt. J.T. Smith, Lt J.A. Howson, 2nd-Lt W.R. Hornby, Lt W. Sames, Lt R.H. Taylor, Lt J.B. Duckworth, Capt. J.B. Polding. Middle row: Lt A. Heard, Lt L. Green, Lt A.F. Behrend, Capt. J.C. Wynne, Lt C. Heywood, Lt R.T. Hunt, Lt A.J.D. Robinson, Lt G. Bennett (QM), Capt. P. Dixon, Lt A.W. Fyldes, Lt M.D. Robinson, Capt. C.St.J. Broadbent. Front row: Capt. E.L. Carus TD, Maj. W.A. Smith (MO), Lt-Col. T.H. Wesley VD, Lt-Col. F.D. Robinson VD (Commanding), Capt. F.M. Livingstone-James (Adjutant), Capt. H. Henry (MO), Capt. B.G. Elliot. (Blackburn)

Soldiers of the 4th Battalion, The East Lancashire Regiment, sharpening their bayonets in Egypt, probably before the Gallipoli campaign of 1915. (Blackburn)

2nd-Lt A.V. Smith, 5th Battalion, The East Lancashire Regiment, son of the Chief Constable of Burnley, who was awarded a posthumous Victoria Cross for a magnificent act of self-sacrifice at Gallipoli. On 23 December 1915 he threw himself on a grenade which was about to detonate in order to save the lives of those around him.

Recruits for the 11th (Service) Battalion, The East Lancashire Regiment, better known as 'The Accrington Pals' on parade on Ellison's Tenement, Accrington, 24 September 1914. The most famous of all the locally recruited 'Pals' battalions, the 11th East Lancashires drew its recruits from Blackburn, Burnley and Chorley as well as Accrington. (Blackburn)

A group of the 'regulars' of the Commercial Hotel, Chorley, celebrate their enlistment into the 'Chorley Pals' Company of 11th (Service) Battalion, The East Lancashire Regiment. (Blackburn)

'Accrington Pals' at a training camp in England, 1915. The Battalion served in Egypt from January to March 1916 and was then transferred to the Western Front where, on 1 July 1916, it was virtually destroyed on the first day of the battle of the Somme, suffering 594 casualties out of a complement of 720.

The 8th East Lancashires, seen here in 1915, were another battalion of Kitchener's 'New Army'. Sailing to France in July 1915, they fought on the Somme and in the Arras and Passchendaele offensives. (Blackburn)

The 3rd Battalion, The East Lancashire Regiment, based near Plymouth, with Headquarters at Laira Battery, for most of the war, was responsible for providing trained drafts of men for the Regular and Service Battalions of the Regiment in the Expeditionary Forces. The Battalion, seen here at a review in 1916, generally had a strength of over 2,000 men.

Ready for service. Over the course of the war over 500 officers and 21,480 other ranks were trained by the 3rd Battalion and drafted to the various battlefronts. Note the Vickers and Lewis machine guns.

Officers of the 3rd Battalion, The East Lancashire Regiment, *c.* 1916. Most of the men seen here were transient, recuperating from wounds or awaiting drafting. They include Capt. J.W. Pendlebury MC (seated, on far right), who later commanded the 1st Battalion at Dunkirk and became Colonel of the Regiment.

'C' Company, 2/4th East Lancashires, on training in England, *c.* 1915. This second-line Battalion of Blackburn Territorials moved to France in February 1917 and, together with the 2/5th East Lancashires from Burnley, saw hard fighting at Passchendaele in October that year when the two battalions suffered nearly 700 casualties. (Blackburn)

Lt-Col. J.E. Green DSO, seen here as a Captain, *c.* 1905, commanded the 1st Battalion, The East Lancashire Regiment, at the Battle of the Somme, where he was wounded. A veteran of the Boer War and the Retreat from Mons, he had the unusual distinction of commanding the 1st Battalion on three separate occasions during the First World War and the 2nd Battalion once. After the war he again commanded the XXXth, from 2 June 1919 to 2 June 1923 when he inaugurated the annual competition between the Officers and Sergeants Messes.

2nd-Lt W. Daly, one of the few East Lancashire officers to survive unscathed the terrible slaughter of 1 July 1916. The 30th suffered 463 casualties on this, the first day of the battle of the Somme. 2nd-Lt Daly enlisted as a private soldier of the 1st Battalion, The East Lancashire Regiment, in 1906. He was commissioned in April 1916 and commanded 'B' Company through the latter stages of the Somme battle, and at Arras and Third Ypres, earning the Military Cross and Bar for his gallant leadership. When the war ended he was commanding the Battalion.

Bombers of the 7th Battalion, The East Lancashire Regiment, going into action at La Boiselle during the Battle of the Somme. On 2/3 July 1916 the Battalion cleared 800yds of German trenches, mainly by bombing.

Cpl Harry Aspinall, one of the original 'Accrington Pals', survived the Somme but was killed in action on 24 March 1918 during stubborn resistance to stem the final German offensive, which cost the Battalion 350 casualties. This photograph was taken on 23 October 1916 when the 'Pals' were again on the Somme, holding trenches near to their ill-fated assault line of 1 July.

Territorials from Blackburn and area forming the 4th Battalion, The East Lancashire Regiment. They are seen in the trenches at Nieuport Bains, Belgium, September 1917. This was the extreme left of the line of Allied trenches extending from the Swiss border to the sea. The Germans were on the far side of the Yser Canal, across which 'swimming patrols' were mounted. Note bayonet-mounted observation mirror. (IWM)

A platoon of the 7th Battalion, The East Lancashire Regiment, marching through Givenchy, 1917.

Capt. N.C. Swift MC of 2nd Battalion, The East Lancashire Regiment, looking debonair amidst the mud at Passchendaele, December 1917. The gallant captain had earned a DSO and a Bar to his MC by the time he was killed leading a counter-attack at Rosieres in March 1918.

Soldiers of the 4th Battalion, The East Lancashire Regiment, manning trenches at Givenchy, January 1918. (IWM)

LCpl William McIver of 2nd Battalion, The East Lancashire Regiment, pictured with his sister Kitty before he went to France. McIver was killed on 27 May 1918 during the second Battle of the Aisne. The Battalion lost double its normal strength in a succession of actions to stem the final German offensive; casualties between 23 March and 1 June 1918 totalled 63 officers and 1,254 men, but two months later the reorganized Battalion was back in the line, remaining in action until the Armistice. (Blackburn)

In Remembrance: in 1922 former Officers of the 4th Battalion, The East Lancashire Regiment, revisited their 1917 trenches at Petit Priot Farm on the Somme. A total of 333 officers and 6,305 men of the East Lancashire Regiment died in the First World War.

Five

1919-1839

The Corps of Drums, 1st Battalion, at St George's Barracks, Malta, in 1924. The silver drums were purchased by past and serving officers of the XXXth in memory of the officers of the Battalion killed during the First World War and were handed over by Field Marshall Lord Plumer, Governor and Commander-in-Chief Malta, at a parade on 4 May 1924.

The NCO i/c Reliefs posting sentries of the 1st Battalion, The East Lancashire Regiment, on Public Duties at Edinburgh Castle, August 1921. Later that year the Battalion sailed for Bermuda and Jamaica, providing garrisons there until 1923 when they moved on to Malta.

The 1st Battalion, The East Lancashire Regiment, presenting arms during their inspection by Lord Plumer on arrival in Malta, where the Battalion was stationed (except for a six-month excursion to Egypt and the Sudan) from 1923 to 1925. The XXXth had a long association with Malta, for it was the Commanding Officer of that Regiment who accepted the keys of Valletta when the French surrendered the island in 1800.

The 2nd Battalion, The East Lancashire Regiment, marching past HM King George V and Queen Mary at the Royal Review on Laffan's Plain, Aldershot, 10 June 1925. After the First World War the Battalion had spent some four years in troubled Ireland, at Buttevant, Londonderry and Carrickfergus, before moving in 1923 to Bordon – their first posting in England since 1897.

A platoon of the 2nd Battalion, The East Lancashire Regiment, with Lewis Guns at Bordon, c. 1923-25. Note the diamond-shaped Regimental flashes on the men's helmets.

Seasonal greetings from Quetta, on the turbulent Baluchistan frontier of India, where the 1st East Lancashires were stationed from 1926 to 1929.

The Sergeants' Mess of the 1st Battalion, The East Lancashire Regiment, at Quetta, June 1926. They are wearing blue No. 1 Dress and regimental side-hats. The great majority are veterans of the First World War.

The winner of the 'Best Machine Gun Mule' at Quetta Horse Show in 1927. Each British Battalion in India at that time had an Indian Platoon wearing its Regimental cap-badge.

King Amanullah of Afghanistan leaves after inspecting the Guard of Honour furnished by 1st Battalion, The East Lancashire Regiment, at the Baluchistan frontier station of Chaman on 10 December 1927. He was at the start of the first state visit to India by an Afghan ruler.

The XXXth on the march during manoeuvres near Quetta, Baluchistan, in 1928. Much of the training in this harsh terrain was for mountain warfare.

A group of 1 Platoon, 'A' Company, 1st East Lancashires, relaxing in camp at Kuchlak, Baluchistan during annual manoeuvres in 1928.

94

Winners of the Quetta Hunt Point to
Point, 1929. Left to right are: Lt T.Mc.I.
Storey, Maj. H.T. McMullen MC, Capt.
R.K. Spurrell of the 1st Battalion, The
East Lancashire Regiment. The $3\frac{1}{2}$ mile
course was completed in a dust storm
and a heat of some 80 degrees in the
shade. The prizes presented on this
occasion, a Silver Fox and a Rose Bowl,
are displayed to this day among the
Regiment's many trophies.

Lt-Col. W.J. Cranston DSO,
Commanding Officer of XXXth (1927-
31) in Quetta, Poona and Bombay. He
was commissioned in 1915 after
eighteen years in the ranks.

Lord Irwin, Viceroy of India, inspecting a Guard of Honour furnished by the 1st Battalion, The East Lancashire Regiment, at the Gateway of India, Bombay, on his departure from India in 1931. The Guard, 100 men commanded by Capt. G.W.V. Hoskyn, drew eulogies from the Viceroy and the Commander-in-Chief for their splendid turn out and bearing. The average height of the Guard was 5ft 11in.

The Corps of Drums and, at rear, Regimental Band of 1st Battalion, The East Lancashire Regiment, on parade at Shanghai Racecourse, c. 1932. Note the silver drums and leopard-skin aprons. The Battalion had made a hurried move from Bombay to Shanghai in March 1932 as part of an multi-national force to protect the International Settlement in that city during the Sino-Japanese clash which was a precursor of the Second World War in the Far East.

The Colours of the XXXth and the 59th met for the first time on the quayside at Shanghai in February 1933 when the 2nd Battalion arrived there aboard HMT *Neuralia* to relieve the 1st Battalion.

Sons of the Regiment, photographed on the meeting of both Battalions in Shanghai, February 1933. Left to right, back row: RSM R.T. Slater (son of RSM A.S. Slater, late 59th), Pte F. Mitchell (son of CSgt W. Mitchell DCM, 2nd Battalion), Boy A.H. Lee (son of WO II A.W. Lee MC, late 59th), LCpl B. Lydon (son of RSM P.T. Lydon DCM, late 30th), LCpl W.W. Edwards (son of S/Sgt J. Edwards, late 30th), Band-Sgt J. Fenner (son of Sgt J. Fenner, late 59th), RSM J.W. Wallace DCM (son of Sgt J. Wallace, late 30th and 59th). Middle row: Lt G.W.B. Stuart (son of Maj. G.R.C. Stuart, late 59th), Lt R.E.D. Green (son of Lt-Col J.E. Green DSO, late 30th and 59th), Lt W.H. Lambert (son of Brig.-Gen. T.S. Lambert CB CMG, late 30th and 59th), Lt L.H.B. Lethbridge (son of Col. R.T.M. Lethbridge OBE, late 30th and 59th), 2nd-Lt W.H.C. Luddington (son of Col. W.J.C. Luddington, late 30th and 59th). Front row: Boy J. Sharples (son of Lt H.S. Sharples MC, late 59th), Dmr J. Spencer (son of CSgt J. Spencer, late 59th), Dmr W. Sharples (son of Lt H.S. Sharples MC, late 59th).

The 2nd Battalion, The East Lancashire Regiment, on the parade ground at Shamshipu Barracks, Kowloon, Hong Kong where the Battalion was stationed from November 1933 to January 1937. The next move was to Ambala in India.

The Boxing Champions of the 2nd Battalion, The East Lancashire Regiment, at Hong Kong, 1936. They are wearing silver trophy belts and the Lilywhites' fleur-de-lys. The two officers in front, wearing black mourning bands for the death of King George V, are, left to right: Capt. J.R. Thatcher and Lt-Col. A.C. Marsh (Commanding). Thatcher was a noted boxer himself, who commanded the 2nd Battalion from 1942 to 1944 at home, in Madagascar, India and Burma until he was wounded in the Arakan. He later commanded the 1st Battalion from 1948 to 1950.

The Colour Company ('D') of the 59th returning the Colours to the Officers' Mess after the Commander-in-Chief's Parade at Ambala, 8 April 1938. The mounted officer on the right is Maj. G.W.P.N. Burden, who subsequently commanded the 1st Battalion (from 1943 to 1944) and earned great distinction in the North-West Europe liberation campaign, while on the left is Capt. C. Jones, the Adjutant, who commanded the Battalion from 1950 to 1952.

A party of HQ Company, 2nd Battalion, led by CSM Elvin, on the bridle path up to Kasauli hill station, 27 April 1938.

Led by the Corps of Drums, 1st Battalion, The East Lancashire Regiment, march into Brebach, near Saarbrucken, on 22 December 1934. The Battalion was in the Saarland as part of a League of Nations force to maintain order during the Saar Plebiscite, held in January 1935 in accordance with the provisions of the Treaty of Versailles, to decide whether the Saar Territory should be returned to Germany.

'B' Company, 1st Battalion, The East Lancashire Regiment, on guard duty at the Wartburg Saal, Saarbrucken, where the votes were counted and the results announced – a victory for Hitler's Germany.

The 1st Battalion, The East
Lancashire Regiment, marching
into Wellington Barracks, London,
on return from the Saar,
28 February 1928.

Maj.-Gen. J.G. Dill CB CMG DSO
(later Field Marshall Sir John Dill),
Colonel of the Regiment, handing
over to Drm-Maj. E. Levett the
silver Drum-Major's Staff presented
to the Regiment by the Sergeants'
Mess of the 1st Battalion as a
memorial to seventy-two of their
members who fell in the First
World War and whose names are
inscribed on the staff. The
ceremony took place at Catterick
Camp, 1935.

In 1936 the 1st Battalion deployed to Egypt with the 5th Division to counter a threatened Italian invasion from Libya. The photograph shows an East Lancashire machine gun post at Sidi Barrani in the Western Desert. The soldiers are wearing goggles because of the prevalent dust storms. Defence spending was a low priority for most of the inter-war years and the Battalion was equipped with ancient machine guns and anti-tank guns that had been withdrawn from the Imperial War Museum.

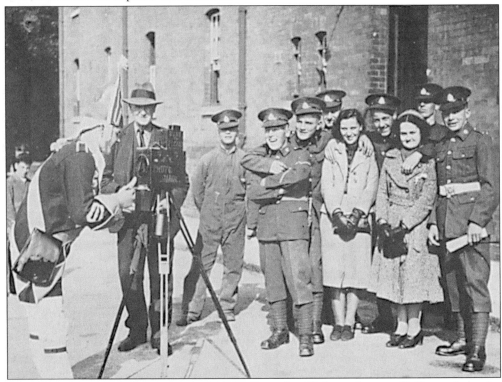

Army Day, 10 September 1938, at Palace Barracks, Holywood, near Belfast, where 1st Battalion, The East Lancashire Regiment, was stationed between 1937 and 1939.

Between the wars there was a major expansion of the Regimental Association. This photograph shows two members of the Burnley Branch. Left to right: Ex-Pte Airey MM and Ex-CSM W. Neill DCM (Branch Secretary).

The Mayor of Preston visited the Depot of the East Lancashire Regiment, Fulwood Barracks, on 12 January 1931, to see recruits under training. Tasting the Irish stew, the Mayor pronounced it 'most excellent'.

Army Day at Fulwood Barracks, 1936. East Lancashire Regiment recruits of Arras Platoon, under Sergeant Hanson, gave a display of 1840s drill and musketry using authentic muzzle-loading weapons.

Anti-gas training for Militia recruits at the East Lancashire Regiment Depot, Fulwood Barracks, in 1938. This was part of the panic expansion of the Armed Forces which immediately preceded the Second World War.

Six
1939-1945

Padiham Territorials of The East Lancashire Regiment march through their home town, *c.* 1939. Between the wars the TA element of the Regiment had been combined as 4th/5th East Lancashires, but as war approached this amalgamation was hastily, if belatedly, reversed and both 4th and 5th Battalions saw active service overseas.

The action of 'B' Company, 1st East Lancashires, on the Bergues Canal, 1 June 1940, when Capt. Marcus Ervine-Andrews earned the only Victoria Cross awarded for the defence of the Dunkirk perimeter. This image was taken from a painting by Frank Wootton which hangs in the Officers' Mess of the 1st Battalion, The Queen's Lancashire Regiment.

Officers of the 1st Battalion, The East Lancashire Regiment, at The Old Priory, Burford, where the XXXth were stationed from September 1943 until moving to join the 53rd Welsh Division on 17 October. Left to right, back row: Lt Carroll, Lt Johnson, Lt R.J. Hawkins, Lt A. Wildgoose, Capt. Coffey Capt. E.C. Griffin MC, Lt Peymon, Lt Tull, Lt Harding. Middle row: Capt. O'Donnell, Capt. H.G. Le Cocq, Capt. E. Allen, Lt J.F. Moore MBE (QM), Capt. B.A. Olley, Capt. H.J. Stockings MC, Lt Greaves, Lt Wyatt, Lt Jeavons, Capt. Cole MC (RAMC). Front row: Maj. C.W. Griffin MC, Maj. Robinson, Maj. Maidment, Lt-Col. G.W.P.N. Burden DSO, Capt. & Adjt C.R. Mitchell, Maj. J.F. Lake MC, Maj. F.O. Cetre MC, Maj. A.T. Bain.

A group of Officers and NCOs of the 5th Battalion, The East Lancashire Regiment, at Folkestone, 1943, including (third from left , second row) Maj. H.M. Ervine-Andrews VC.

The Mortar Platoon, 1st Battalion, The East Lancashire Regiment, May 1944. Left to right, back row: Pte Cooper, Pte Hodge, Pte Snape, Pte E. Ashley, Pte Moye, Pte J. Orrell, Pte R. Bamber, Sgt Hall, Pte Earle, Pte J. Pettifer, Pte McBrearty. Pte Rothwell. Second row from the back: Pte Marsden, Pte Burton, Pte Dewhurst, Pte Yump, Pte A. Roberts, Pte E. Griffiths, Pte Hurst, Pte A. Towers, Pte Bailey, Cpl Petre. Third row: Cpl Seedhall, L/Sgt L. Lacey, L/Sgt Cavanagh, Sgt Stott, Sgt McFarland, Capt. H.A. Tull, Sgt Mellor, Cpl L. Beddows, LCpl Rone. Front row: Pte Bradley, Pte Ashton, Pte Godwin, Pte Whalley, Pte Kneale, Pte Wright, Pte Todd, Pte Blower.

The Carrier Platoon, 1st Battalion, The East Lancashire Regiment, May 1944. 'I wish I had two such Carrier Platoons' said Col. Burden on more than one occasion of this highly-trained and very mobile sub-unit.

By the end of June 1944 both the 1st and 5th Battalions of the East Lancashire Regiment had landed in Normandy for the liberation of Europe. This photograph shows an East Lancashire Regiment carrying party, probably from the 5th Battalion, near Villers-Bocage. (IWM)

On 12 August 1944 the 1st East Lancashires, in their first major action of the campaign, captured the village of Bois Halbout in a remarkably effective quick attack and held it against a strong enemy counter-attack. On 12 August 1998 the Regimental Association returned to 'Boiled Halibut', as the Lancashire soldiers styled the little town, to unveil a memorial to all their comrades who had fallen in North-West Europe. At the unveiling ceremony above were, left to right: Ex-Cpl R. Atkinson, Ex-Pte T. Neary, Lt-Col Cetre MC (all veterans of the battle) and the Mayor of Blackburn.

In 1941 the 8th Battalion, The East Lancashire Regiment, was converted to armour and retitled 144th Regiment Royal Armoured Corps. As such it fought in Normandy (where this picture was taken, near Caen, on 8 July 1944) in Holland, the Ardennes and Germany with conspicuous success. On 1 March 1945 it had the honour of being selected to become a Regular regiment and was again renamed as 4th Royal Tank Regiment.

In early September, having advanced from Normandy into Belgium with little opposition, the East Lancashires were diverted to assist in clearing the vital docks at Antwerp. In this picture a 6-pounder anti-tank gun of the 1st Battalion, The East Lancashire Regiment, is covering the approaches to the docks. (IWM)

On the night 16/17 September 1944, as part of Operation Market Garden, the 1st East Lancashires made a difficult but completely successful assault crossing of the Meuse-Escaut Canal at Lommel on the border between Belgium and Holland. Here the Commanding Officer's carrier can be seen moving down to the left rafting site. He is followed by Capt. E.C. Griffin MC who, with Maj. Lake and Capt. Le Cocq, had plunged into the canal in the dark to rescue men from two boats sunk in the assault.

Sgt H. Bradbury MM and his anti-tank gun crew of the 1st East Lancashires in action against German tanks and SP guns at s'Hertogenbosch, Holland, 26 October 1944. Left to right: Cpl Johnson MM (and French Croix de Guerre), Pte Carter, Sgt Bradbury MM, Pte Addis. (IWM)

The 1st East Lancashires advancing through s'Hertogenbosch, October 1944. The capture of this ancient town, surrounded by flooded polders and intersected with canals, was a formidable task and involved the East Lancashires in a daring, and brilliantly successful, night attack along a railway causeway followed by assault crossings of the canals and street fighting to clear strong German opposition. (IWM)

Advancing across the North German Plain, the 1st East Lancashires took part in the capture of Hamburg, 4 May 1945, their last operation of the war. In ten months of almost constant fighting the Battalion had suffered 1,296 battle casualties, including 20 officers and 241 men killed in action. Losses had, as ever, fallen most heavily on the rifle companies. Only 71 of their soldiers who had landed in Normany were still present on VE Day, including the NCOs and men of 'D' Company shown here. Left to right, back row: WO II (CSM) C. Payne MM, LCpl E. Davies, LCpl J. Stringfellow LCpl G. Oakley, Pte J. Fisher, Pte Briggs, Pte R.E. Brock, Pte Keighley, Pte A. Turner, Pte Bowers, Sgt D. Thomas, LCpl W. Garton, LCpl H. Harrison. Front row, sitting: Cpl W. Entwistle, Cpl Marsden, L/Sgt J. Oram MM, L.Sgt Wride MM, Sgt C. Atkins MM, Sgt Richards, Cpl Ormerod, Cpl Garth, Cpl C. Woods, LCpl A. Turner.

The Sergeants' Mess, 2nd Battalion, The East Lancashire Regiment, at Ahmedabad, India, in 1943 when the Battalion was training for jungle warfare in Burma. Left to right, back row: Band-Sgt J. Sale, Sgt G. Marks, Sgt J. Richardson, Sgt C.P. Lambert MM, Sgt F. Benson, Sgt R. Robinson, Sgt N. Sheppard, L/Sgt R. Hargreaves, L/Sgt G. Hickey, Sgt-Clerk H. Buxton, L/Sgt J. Woodhead, L/Sgt J. Prince, L/Sgt E. Shove RAOC, Sgt W. Dutton. Second row from the back: Sgt J. Heyes, Sgt L. Surridge, L/Sgt N. Booth, L/Sgt W. Walkden, Sgt J. Walsh, Sgt H. Emmerson, Sgt H. Raby, Sgt H. Preston, L/Sgt C. Hardy, L/Sgt W. Wynne, Sgt C. Barrett, L/Sgt N. Langford, Pioneer-Sgt F. Atkins, L/Sgt S. Evans. Third row: Armourer-Sgt W. Tew RAOC, Sgt J. Derbyshire, Sgt C. Pratt, Sgt G. Ellison, Sgt W. Sharples, Sgt R. Lewis, Sgt G. Idiens, Sgt D. Williams, Sgt C. Vasper, Sgt F. Mulvey, Sgt A. Fildes, Sgt J. Corcoran, L/Sgt A. Parry, Sgt C. Calverley, L/Sgt F. Brown. Fourth row: L/Sgt B. Badman, Sgt J. Smalley, L/Sgt J. Curtis, CSgt F. Coward, CSgt H. Almond, CSgt E. Goodfellow, CSgt C. Lane, CSgt R. Gunner, CSgt W. Dorothy, Sgt G. Dalgleish, Sgt A. Taylor, Sgt J. Pollard, Fitter-Sgt S. Hannon REME, L/Sgt B. Smith. Front row, seated: WO II (CSM) A. Thornton, WO II F. Cheadle, WO II L. Wilson, Maj. T.A. Eccles (second-in-Command), RSM A. Goodwin, Lt-Col. J.R. Thatcher (Commanding), RQMS S. Henchy, Capt. B.H. Woods (Adjutant), WO II (CSM) C. Hensey, Lt & QM T. O'Malley, WO II (CSM) J. Bowers, WO II J. Chaplin.

A casualty arrives at the Regimental Aid Post belonging to the 2nd Battalion, The East Lancashire Regiment, in the dense jungle of the Mayu Ridge in the Arakan, February 1944. The Battalion fought there as part of the 36th Division.

'B' Company, 2nd Battalion, The East Lancashire Regiment, crossing a chaung during their advance on Mohnyin, Burma, October 1944.

A patrol of the 2nd East Lancashires advances through razor edge grass and swamp on the way to Mohnyin. Villages were often fortresses of Japanese resistance and, on 25 August 1944, the Battalion had fought a major engagement to capture the village of Inyingon.

Men of the 2nd Battalion, The East Lancashire Regiment, rafting equipment across the Schweli River, Burma, December 1944.

A company of 2nd Battalion, The East Lancashire Regiment, searching the jungle for Japanese snipers, Burma.

The Officers of the 2nd Battalion, The East Lancashire Regiment, at Mongmit, Burma, February 1945. Left to right, back row: Lt H. Marsden, Lt P.C.A.L. Buer, Lt E. Prince, Lt P. Curry, Lt R. Parry-Evans, Lt J.H. Selby, Lt S.B. Taylor, Lt T.H. Worthington, Lt P.N. Slater, Lt J. Crook, Lt H.R. Rowntree MBE, Lt P. Grimshaw, Lt G.A. Marr. Middle row: Lt D.K. Allen, Lt R.F. Chilton, Lt J. Thompson, Lt D.L. McRae, Capt. H.J. Kirk, Capt. R.C. Ashcroft MC, Capt. T. O'Malley (QM), Capt. C. Leeming, Capt. J.A. Brown, Capt. D. Short (RMO), Lt D. Rigden, Lt H.R. Derby. Front row: Maj. A.W. Gossage, Maj. F.J.H. Arnold MC, Maj. R. Green, Maj. A.T. Chamberlayne, Lt-Col. T.A. Eccles OBE, Capt. L.W. Williams, Maj. M.L.D. Skewes-Cox, Maj. B.H. Woods MBE, Maj. W.S. Adam MC.

Lt-Col. Eccles holds his last 'Orders' Group of the Burma campaign on the Kalaw Road, May 1945. On 15 May the 59th left from Meiktila for India, where the Battalion was stationed at Dinapore.

116

Seven
1945-1958

Farewell to India in 1947. Earl Mountbatten of Burma, the last Viceroy of India, saluting the Colours of the 2nd Battalion, The East Lancashire Regiment, at the Farewell Parade in New Delhi. The 59th sailed from Bombay on 28 December 1947, over 141 years after the Regiment's first service in India, and returned to England for amalgamation with the 1st Battalion.

On 28 June 1947 there was a ceremony (Operation 'Puffer') at Preston railway station to mark the naming of LMS Engine No. 6135 as *The East Lancashire Regiment*. The unveiling was carried out by Brig. J.W. Pendlebury DSO MC, Colonel of the Regiment, and Sir Robert Burrows, Chairman of the LMS Railway Company. Today a replica of this nameplate hangs outside the guardroom of the 1st Battalion, The Queen's Lancashire Regiment.

The Return of the Eagle. On 28 September 1947, at the Royal Hospital, Chelsea, the Eagle of the French 22nd Regiment, captured at the battle of Salamanca in 1812 by Ensign Pratt of the XXXth Regiment, was returned to the East Lancashire Regiment. The 1st Battalion escort, commanded by Maj. T.A. Eccles OBE, is seen here marching past the Governor of the Royal Hospital and the Colonel of the Regiment.

Brig. J.W. Pendlebury DSO MC, Colonel of the Regiment, inspecting the ancient Regimental Colour of the XXX at Fulwood Barracks, Preston, 16 April 1948. The Colours had been laid up for safe keeping in Burnley parish church for the duration of the Second World War.

Disbanded in Egypt in November 1946 after a period of garrison service in the Middle East, the 4th Battalion was re-born at its old home, Canterbury Street, Blackburn, on 1 May 1947 as part of the reconstituted Territorial Army. Signing on are, left to right: Mr Palmer, Mt Busby and Mr Chippendale, with RSM P. O'Reilley, Capt. J.A. Underwood and Capt. (QM) H.H. Snaith MBE TD.

The 1st Battalion, The East Lancashire Regiment, marching through Blackburn 'with drums beating, bands playing, Colours flying and bayonets fixed' when the Regiment received the Freedom of the Borough, 17 April 1948. The parade also included contingents from the 2nd and 4th Battalions, the Home Guard, the Cadet Force and some six hundred Old Comrades.

The Regimental Colours of all three battalions of The East Lancashire Regiment at Canterbury Street Barracks before the Freedom of Blackburn Parade, 17 April 1948. Left to right, from the 1st Battalion: WO II (CSM) R. Lewis, Capt. P. Callaghan, WO II (CSM) C. Payne MM. From the 2nd Battalion: WO II (CSM) A.J. Howell, Capt. I.F.C. Shepherd, WO II (CSM) A.E. Taylor. From the 4th Battalion: WO II (CSM) C. O'Malley, Capt. J.F. Thornton, Sgt J. Merrick.

The Regimental Band of the East Lancashire Regiment at Hadrian's Camp, Carlisle, where, on 17 September 1948, the old XXXth and 59th were formally amalgamated. The Regiment's long-serving Bandmaster, WO I Moore, is seated centre.

The Presentation of Colours to 1st Battalion, The East Lancashire Regiment, by Lord Derby at Chester in 1950, showing 2nd-Lt Frier receiving the Regimental Colour watched by Lt-Col Thatcher.

Capt. E.C. Griffin MC, Adjutant of the 4th Battalion, The East Lancashire Regiment, conducting a cloth model tactical exercise at Canterbury Street Barracks, Blackburn, 1949.

The ceremony outside Burnley Town Hall when, on 6 June 1953, the Borough granted its Freedom to The East Lancashire Regiment. This honour was conferred in connection with the Coronation of HM Queen Elizabeth II, which took place the same week, and in appreciation of the great achievements, distinguished record and glorious traditions of the Regiment in which so many Burnley men had been proud to serve.

The Regimental Band and Corps of Drums, 1st Battalion, The East Lancashire Regiment, at the Governor-General's Palace, Khartoum, in 1951. The Battalion was stationed in the Sudan, at Khartoum and Gebeit, from 1950 until 1951 when it moved to the unsettled Canal Zone of Egypt for internal security duties.

The Mortar Platoon of the 1st Battalion, The East Lancashire Regiment, coming into action in Egypt, c. 1952. Despite the terrorist threat, large-scale conventional exercises were held in the rugged desert training areas.

Drum-Major Noble leading the 4th Battalion, The East Lancashire Regiment, from Canterbury Street Barracks to entrain at Blackburn station on their way to the 42nd Division Camp on Salisbury Plain, August 1953, which included exercises at battalion, brigade and divisional level. On such occasions the Battalion was accustomed to march from their drill hall past the Town Hall, where the Mayor took the salute.

On 27 October 1953, to the sound of cheering soldiers and the music of the Regimental Band, the 1st East Lancashires sailed into Southampton on the *Empire Ken* at the end of a three and a half-year tour in the Middle East. They were met by the Mayors of Blackburn (left) and Burnley, who are seen here with the Colonel of the Regiment and Lt-Col. C.C.S. Genese, the Commanding Officer.

In 1954 the 1st Battalion moved to Germany and joined the Rhine Army, stationed first at Gort Barracks, Hubbelrath, as part of the 4th Guards Brigade of 2nd Division and then in Alma Barracks, Luneburg, as lorried Infantry with 7th Armoured Division. This photograph shows Cpl Taylor and Pte Smalley of the Signal Platoon on exercise in October 1954. The following year Battle Dress was replaced as a field uniform when the Battalion carried out troop trials of the new olive drab Combat Clothing.

Maj.-Gen. W.H. Lambert CB CBE, the last Colonel of The East Lancashire Regiment, on the steps of the Depot Officers' Mess at Fulwood Barracks, Preston on Somme Day 1957.

The last photograph of the Officers of the 1st Battalion, The East Lancashire Regiment, in Hong Kong prior to the 1958 amalgamation. Left to right, back row: 2nd-Lt R.K. Evans, 2nd-Lt R.C. Cartwright, 2nd-Lt P.J. Shepherd, 2nd-Lt J.M. Cunningham, 2nd-Lt S.G. Harrison, 2nd-Lt R.N. Hopwood, 2nd-Lt K.J. Ainsworth. Second row from the back: 2nd-Lt R.P. Carrington, Lt G.M. Cattermole, Lt H.G. Richardson, Lt C. Gately, Lt A.J. Ostrowski, Lt L.F.E. Fitzpatrick-Robertson, 2nd-Lt O.W. Speight. Third row: Capt. (QM) H. Almond, Lt N.J. Allen, Capt. I.V.C. Frier, Capt. D. Smith, Capt. R.T. Smith, Lt T.C.W. Proffitt, Capt. D.M. Linklater RAMC, Lt (QM) J. Kenny. Front row: Maj. A.C.K. Skelcher MBE RAPC, Maj. M.L.D. Skewes-Cox, Maj. C.E. Knight, Maj. F.O. Cetre MC, Lt-Col. C.W. Griffin MC, Capt. P.H.B. O'Meara (Adjutant), Maj. J.M.B. Arrigo, Maj. P.L. Flatman, Capt. J.C. Shaw MBE.

On Somme Day, 1 July 1958, the 1st Battalions of The East Lancashire Regiment and The South Lancashire Regiment (Prince of Wales's Volunteers) amalgamated at Hong Kong to form The Lancashire Regiment (Prince of Wales's Volunteers). The photograph shows the old Colours of both Regiments being handed by the RSM to the Ensigns prior to being trooped for the last time. The East Lancashires' Colours (closest) were carried by Lt Proffitt and 2nd-Lt Hopwood.

The 4th East Lancashires, seen here on their way to weekend training in 1959, remained in existence for a further ten years and are today represented in the Territorial Army order of battle by Somme Company, badged to The Queen's Lancashire Regiment and based in Blackburn.

On 18 April 1964 the Borough of Haslingden granted its Freedom to The East Lancashire Regiment. The 4th Battalion, commanded by Lt-Col. M.L.D. Skewes-Cox, was on parade, as were the Regiment's Cadets and a contingent of Old Comrades.

Somme Sunday 2000 in the Chapel of The East Lancashire Regiment, Blackburn Cathedral. The values and traditions of the old County Regiments are cherished today by their successors of The Queen's Lancashire Regiment.